Turbulence Ahead

Ahead

Contents

Features

Where in the world does the most rain fall? The answer on page 8 might surprise you!

Why are hurricanes sometimes called cyclones or typhoons? Look for the answer on page 15.

Can you imagine what it would be like to fly into the middle of a hurricane? See **Hunting Hurricanes** on page 16.

Have you ever seen a hailstone bigger than a tennis ball? Take a look at **Emergency!** on page 20.

Where in the world are the wildest tornadoes?

Visit **www.rigbyinfoquest.com**
for more about **WEATHER**.

Wet, Wild, and Windy

Weather affects everything on Earth. It changes the land and affects our food supply, the way we live, what we wear, and even how we feel.

Turbulent weather affects us most of all. A sudden storm can ruin crops and damage property. Heavy snow can trap people in their homes for hours or days at a time. Strong winds can blow down trees and affect sea and air travel. A farmer's complete harvest can be destroyed by too much or too little rain.

Fasten your seatbelts. There's turbulence ahead!

Cloud Formations

Clouds are masses of water droplets or ice crystals that float in the sky. Clouds are formed when air with a lot of **water vapor** rises and becomes colder. Cold air can't hold as much water vapor as warm air, so some of the water vapor forms into tiny water droplets or ice crystals around specks of dust in the air. These droplets make up clouds.

When air masses of different temperatures meet, the warmer one rises over the colder one because it is lighter. It cools and clouds form between the air masses.

When air is forced to rise, it cools quickly and clouds are formed.

Clouds look white because water droplets and ice crystals reflect light. A cloud appears dark when it has become so thick that sunlight can no longer pass through it.

When air is warmed over an area of hot ground, it rises. As the rising air cools, it forms towering clouds.

Warm air is forced upward when it meets a mountain range. As the rising air cools, it forms clouds on the windy side of the mountains.

Rain, Hail, and Snow

Rain, hail, and snow are different forms of water that fall from a cloud. They are called **precipitation.** The kind of precipitation that will fall depends mainly on the temperature of the air.

If the temperature is below freezing, clouds form ice crystals instead of water droplets. As the ice crystals grow, they become heavy and fall as snowflakes. If rain passes through a layer of cold air as it falls, the raindrops may freeze and form small pieces of ice, or sleet.

FAST FACTS

The highest rainfall in the world is at Mount Waialeale in Hawaii. About 460 inches of rain fall every year. The lowest rainfall is in Arica, Chile. This desert town receives only 0.03 inches a year.

NORTH AMERICA

Hawaii

SOUTH AMERICA

Arica

Chile

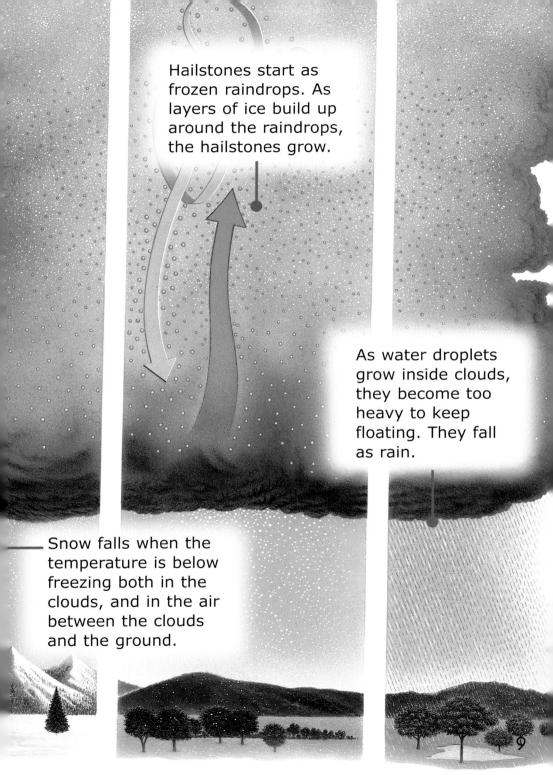

Hailstones start as frozen raindrops. As layers of ice build up around the raindrops, the hailstones grow.

As water droplets grow inside clouds, they become too heavy to keep floating. They fall as rain.

Snow falls when the temperature is below freezing both in the clouds, and in the air between the clouds and the ground.

9

Measuring Rain

A funnel and a narrow tube can be used to collect and measure rain. A radar system can also measure rain. An antenna sends out radio waves that reflect from raindrops. The strength of the reflection is measured—the stronger the waves, the heavier the rainfall.

Floods

Some coastal floods happen when strong winds force high waves onto the land. Heavy rain can cause rivers to overflow their banks and flood surrounding lowlands. Flash floods happen suddenly when heavy rain falls in deep valleys such as canyons.

Storms and heavy rain caused the 1993 Mississippi River flood.

The Coast Guard rescued many people and animals.

You can measure rain by placing a can outside to collect rainwater. Measure the rainwater at the same time each day.

Local people helped fill sandbags.

People used sandbags to stop the flow of water.

Thunder and Lightning

Thunderclouds form on hot, **humid** days. Inside the clouds, water droplets and ice crystals rub together making positive and negative electric charges. Lightning is a flash of light in the sky that happens when there is a sudden flow of electricity between the charges. Thunder is caused by the sudden heating of the air as the electricity passes through it.

Thunder and lightning happen at the same time but light travels faster than sound. We see the lightning first. Then we hear the clap of thunder.

Kinds of Lightning

Cloud to Ground
Lightning forms when there is a buildup of negative charges at the bottom of a cloud and positive charges on the ground below.

Cloud to Cloud
Lightning forms between two clouds when one is negatively charged and the other is positively charged.

Inside a Cloud
Most lightning forms
inside a cloud where
there are both positive
and negative charges.

13

Moving Air

When air moves across the surface of Earth, it is called wind. Winds can vary in strength from a gentle cooling breeze to a wild blasting wind.

Air begins to move when the sun heats parts of the land. The air above these spots becomes warm and light and begins to rise. In other areas, cool air sinks because it is heavier. The wind blows because air that is pushed away by the sinking cold air is sucked under the rising warm air.

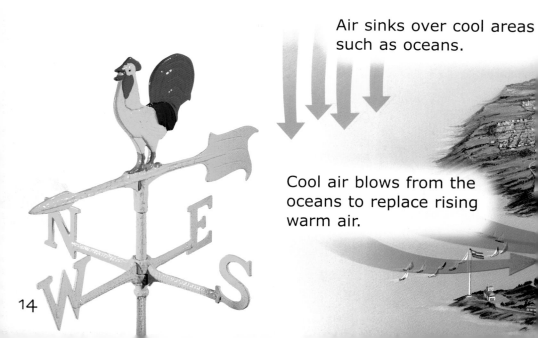

Air sinks over cool areas such as oceans.

Cool air blows from the oceans to replace rising warm air.

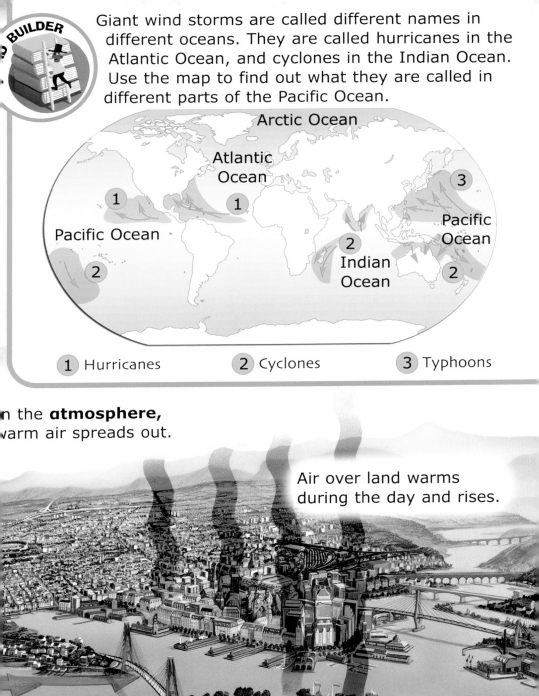

BUILDER

Giant wind storms are called different names in different oceans. They are called hurricanes in the Atlantic Ocean, and cyclones in the Indian Ocean. Use the map to find out what they are called in different parts of the Pacific Ocean.

Arctic Ocean

Atlantic Ocean

Pacific Ocean

Indian Ocean

Pacific Ocean

1 Hurricanes   2 Cyclones   3 Typhoons

n the **atmosphere,**
warm air spreads out.

Air over land warms during the day and rises.

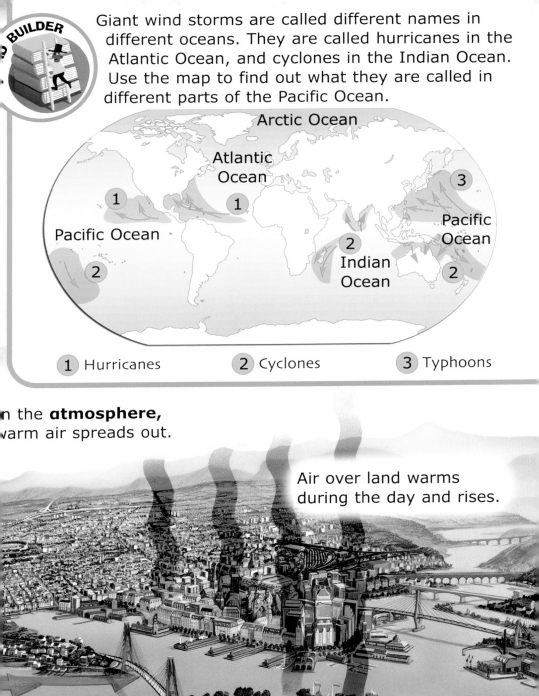

Hunting Hurricanes

What is a hurricane hunter? A pilot from the 53rd Weather Reconnaissance Squadron tells us what hurricane hunters do and where they fly their airplanes!

Q Where do you fly your airplanes?

A Believe it or not, we fly right into the middle of hurricanes and storms.

Q Why do you do this?

A We take measurements of air pressure, temperature, humidity, and wind speed.

Q How do you take these measurements?

A We drop a special instrument called a dropsonde. It records the information we need and then radios it back to the airplane. Our weather officer then sends the information to the United States National Hurricane Center in Florida.

Q Why is the information sent to the Hurricane Center?

A The Center can then warn people who may be in the path of the storm.

Q How many people are on each flight?

A There are six crew members on each flight.

Q How long does each flight last?

A We are in the air for about ten to thirteen hours.

Q Do you follow the storm?

A No. If possible, we fly ahead of the storm. This means the information we collect can be used to warn people who must protect themselves and their property.

Being inside the middle, or eye, of a hurricane is like floating in the middle of a giant football stadium made of clouds. Banks of clouds rise up around us. Clear blue sky is above the airplane. Flying out the other side, however, means going through the second half of the storm!

Extreme Weather

Extreme weather conditions cause disasters all over the world. A tornado is a twisting whirlwind that sucks everything up as it races along the ground. Then it dumps everything down again.

Too much heavy rain can cause a river to overflow its banks and flood the surrounding land. A drought, caused by too little rain, can completely ruin a farmer's crops. Fires that start in hot, dry areas can spread quickly, especially when there are strong winds.

The strong winds that spiral around the eye of a tornado can reach speeds of up to 250 miles per hour. Sometimes, tornadoes pick up large objects, such as cars or houses, and then set them down unharmed nearby.

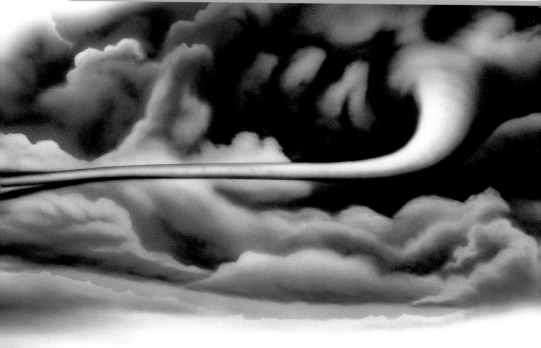

SITESEEING · WATER, EARTH, & SKY

Where in the world are the wildest tornadoes?

Visit **www.rigbyinfoquest.com**
for more about **WEATHER.**

Emergency!

Hundreds of cars parked on Sydney's city streets were hit by huge hailstones.

People living in Sydney, Australia were shocked by a sudden and fierce hailstorm last night. There was no official warning for the storm, which caused millions of dollars worth of damage to property.

The storm began to form south of Sydney, at Nowra, in the late afternoon. The Regional Forecasting Center in Sydney tracked the storm, but forecasters believed it would weaken and move out to sea.

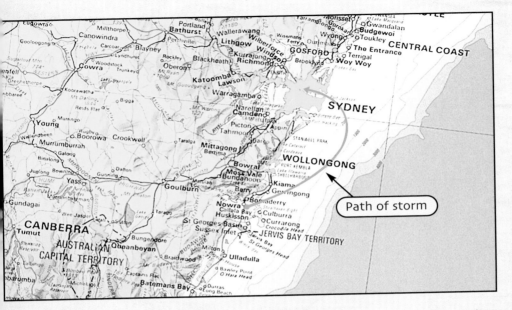

SYDNEY

WOLLONGONG

CENTRAL COAST

GOSFORD

CANBERRA

Path of storm

However, they were wrong. The storm gained power. It moved north and began to produce hail. It reached Sydney Airport and moved inland. By now, it had become an unusual kind of storm called a supercell.

The storm swept across the city, lasting for more than five hours. Hailstones larger than three and a half inches around crashed into houses and cars, smashing through glass and denting rooftops.

Left: Hailstones larger than tennis balls fell during the storm. Compare the size of these hailstones to a coin.

Forecasting Today

People use ships, airplanes, satellites, and special weather stations to help them record the weather every day. **Meteorologists** use the recorded information to make weather maps. Weather maps show information about wind, clouds, temperature, air pressure, and humidity.

Meteorologists study both weather maps and satellite photographs so that they can produce a weather forecast. The weather forecast can show what the weather conditions are likely to be in a few hours or during the days ahead.

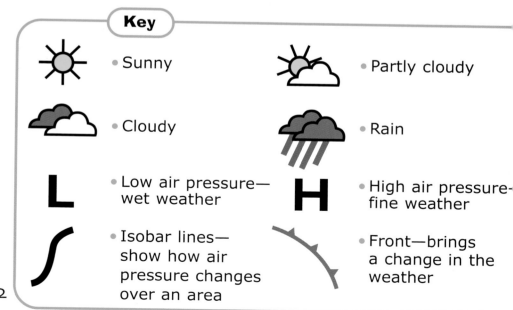

Key

- Sunny
- Cloudy
- Low air pressure— wet weather
- Isobar lines— show how air pressure changes over an area
- Partly cloudy
- Rain
- High air pressure— fine weather
- Front—brings a change in the weather

It is important that all information is carefully recorded to make sure the weather map is as correct as possible.

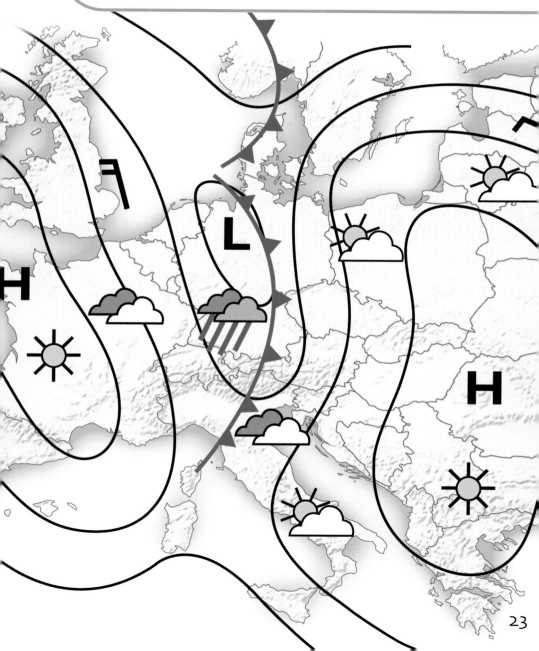

Forecasting by Nature

The weather has always been important to people. Before forecasting became a science, people tried to explain weather patterns through stories or by looking for signs, or clues, in nature. Some told stories of storm gods. Some looked at the color of the sky and the behavior of animals.

Not all signs were right, but some were good enough to help people plan the planting of crops. Today, you can still get an idea of what the weather will be like by looking at the sky.

A Chinese myth tells how a group of gods make a thunderstorm. The Thunder God bangs his drums. The Master of Rain sprinkles water with a sword. The Earl of Wind sends out strong winds from his goatskin bag. Mother Lightning makes lightning with mirrors, and clouds are piled up by The Little Boy of the Clouds.

Signs in Nature

Signs of Fine Weather

busy bees

open morning-glory flowers

open pinecone scales

red sky at night

Signs of Rain

a donkey swaying
and nodding its head

a cat washing itself

dragonflies hovering
just above the ground

pairs of African
guinea fowl
building a nest

World Climates

The climate of an area is the usual condition of the weather throughout the year. It is figured out after studying the temperature and the amount of rain over more than 30 years.

World Climate Zones

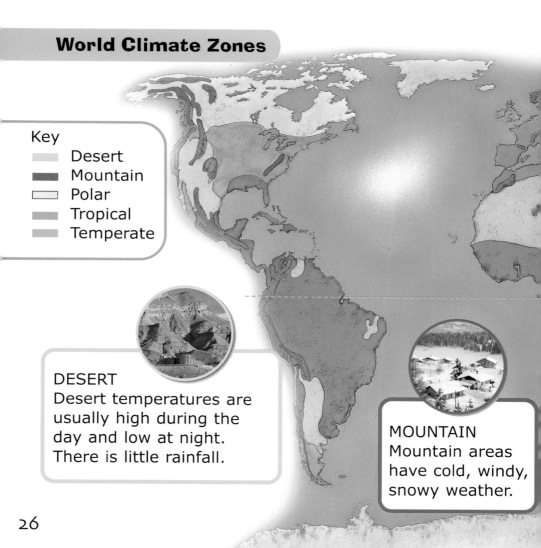

Key
- Desert
- Mountain
- Polar
- Tropical
- Temperate

DESERT
Desert temperatures are usually high during the day and low at night. There is little rainfall.

MOUNTAIN
Mountain areas have cold, windy, snowy weather.

Earth's **spherical** shape is one of the reasons for differences in climate. The sun's energy hits Earth unevenly. More energy from the sun arrives in areas near the equator than near the poles. The climate of any area depends on its location between the equator and the poles, its distance from the sea, and its surrounding landforms.

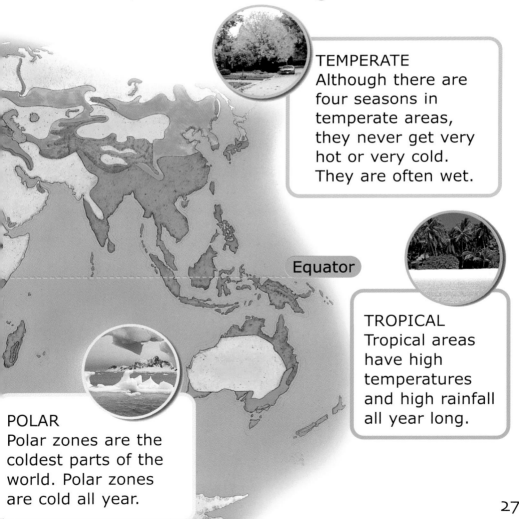

TEMPERATE
Although there are four seasons in temperate areas, they never get very hot or very cold. They are often wet.

Equator

TROPICAL
Tropical areas have high temperatures and high rainfall all year long.

POLAR
Polar zones are the coldest parts of the world. Polar zones are cold all year.

Environmental Issues

The **ozone layer** in the atmosphere protects Earth from the sun's harmful rays. A hole in the ozone layer was found over Antarctica in the 1970s. It is caused by gases and chemicals that escape into the atmosphere. Harmful rays reaching Earth's surface can increase people's risk of skin cancers.

As the quantity of gases from burning coal and oil increases in the atmosphere, Earth's warmth is trapped. This is called global warming. It can cause farmland to become desert, and icy areas to melt and flood surrounding lowlands.

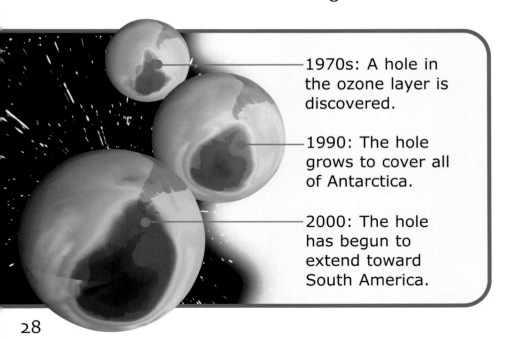

1970s: A hole in the ozone layer is discovered.

1990: The hole grows to cover all of Antarctica.

2000: The hole has begun to extend toward South America.

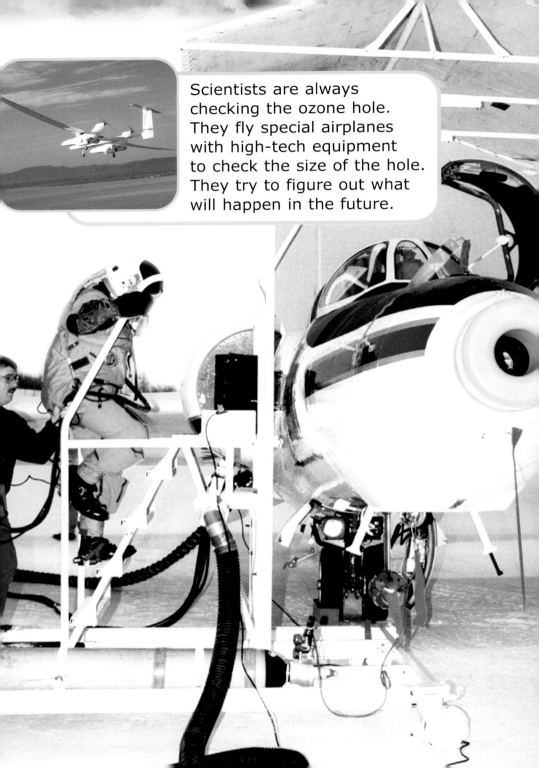

Scientists are always checking the ozone hole. They fly special airplanes with high-tech equipment to check the size of the hole. They try to figure out what will happen in the future.

Glossary

atmosphere – a layer of air that surrounds Earth

humid – a word that describes damp, moist weather conditions

meteorologist – a scientist who studies and predicts the weather

ozone layer – a layer of ozone gas, which is a form of oxygen, high above Earth. The ozone layer blocks out some of the sun's harmful rays.

precipitation – rain, hail, snow, or any other moisture that falls from the sky

spherical – round in shape. All points on the edge of a sphere are the same distance from the center.

turbulent – a word that describes something moving unsteadily or strongly. Turbulent weather can include wild winds, heavy rain, thunder, and lightning.

water vapor – the gas-like form of water. Water becomes vapor when it is evaporated by heat from the sun or when it is boiled. Steam is a kind of water vapor.

Index

Discussion Starters

1 Warm, sunny days often help people feel happier than cold, wet days. Can you remember a day when the weather helped you feel happy? What did you do on that day? What might you have done if the weather was the opposite?

2 When airplanes fly through clouds, the ride can be bumpy. What makes turbulence inside clouds? Do you think you would feel any bumps on a cloudless day? Why or why not?

3 Scientists are worried about how global warming is changing the weather around the world. What kind of efforts might you make in your everyday life that could help stop the changes? Can you name any groups working to help protect Earth from these harmful changes?